Sue,
Follow your road to balance!

Debbie Lessin

Dedication

For my treasured friends.
You sustain me. You make me laugh.
My life is filled with wonder because you
are part of it!

Acknowledgments

All authors have a supporting cast to which many thanks are due.

To Janet Jaffke – your talent is immense; your illustrations have made my words dance and come to life.

To Ida Bialik and Bev Zadikoff, my unofficial Balancing Act Productions, Inc. Board of Directors and friends extraordinaire – you have always believed in my dreams and supported me in achieving them.

To my Family – our circle of love goes round and round, from generation to generation. We are all different, yet we are a family; loving, doing, and being!

To my Readers – thank you for welcoming me into your life!

Contents

Act II - Friends & Family

Act III – Heart & Soul

Act IV - Mind & Body

Epilogue - Your Balancing Activities

The Balancing Act

Time is a precious commodity in this fast paced modern world in which we live. Endless to-do lists have each of us juggling work and play, friends and family, heart and soul, and mind and body in continuously changing cycles. We constantly search for equilibrium in our existence: a balance of sorts. In spite of this effort, this quest occasionally seems like an exercise in futility, and sometimes it is! Finding balance in life requires making and accepting changes. Change is not always easy to initiate or accomplish. To best achieve balance in your life, you must take it one step at a time, and baby steps at that!

My personal quest for life balance began eight years ago, just as I turned forty. As an over-achieving successful entrepreneur, I seriously began questioning why I was working so hard. Money wasn't my primary motivation once the debt to grow the business was finally paid off. I had built a successful accounting practice over ten years that exceeded even my own "type A" expectations.

I was making a comfortable living, which provided me with a nice upscale urban lifestyle in Chicago. I had grown my business and subsequently downsized it (three times in fact!); I learned from experience that bigger wasn't necessarily better. The thrills of the start-up phase were long gone, the heartaches and headaches of growth a fading memory. The burning flames of my professional passion had long ago been extinguished. And despite the comfort and security that came with prolonged entrepreneurial survival, I found myself second-guessing where my life was headed. Something important to my personal happiness was clearly still missing. The flexibility that I had always envisioned as a benefit of owning my own business was sorely lacking. I needed to figure out how to work less, play more, and work smarter! So I methodically began the challenge of balancing my life, one step at a time.

The changes in the past eight years have been simply amazing. Work-wise, I know my busy times and plan my schedule accordingly. I figured out that work would always expand to fill available time. As I became better organized, I needed less time to get my work done. Knowing how and when I worked best was key.

I eliminated unnecessary meetings and scheduled convenient telephone conferences instead. As a CPA, I work very hard and put in long hours during tax season. But I know my physical and mental limitations. I have never burned the midnight oil or pulled an all-nighter. I now only work on Saturdays from mid-February through April 15th. After tax season ends, I reward myself the rest of the year by working three or four days a week at the most and many shortened days at that. Did this happen overnight? Absolutely not. I began slowly with a weekend off here, a few four-day workweeks there. And as I realized that the work still got done in a timely fashion, each succeeding year, I allowed myself to work a little less by working a lot smarter.

Thus, I have added time to have a life beyond work. For me, it is my circle of friends that add the most balance to my life. I have a loving family that is supportive of me in every way. I am lucky in that regard and I know it. My friends are the people I love by choice. Being a good friend is my best character trait; I am proud of that. Dinners, movies, theatre, shopping, talking, and sharing; living our lives in parallel motion despite our non-linear lives. We are there for one another even if we live miles and miles apart.

Sometimes, it is the little pleasures that bring me the most balance and the greatest joy. Walking through my urban garden, gazing at the colorful flowers while the frog fountain spews its watery gurgles of music in the background. Curling up on the couch with a good book in hand - reading feverishly, excited to share this new find with my circle of book friends.

And then there are the kids. While I am not a parent, my nieces and nephews are a big part of my life. Baby Ava is just beginning to talk. Her non-verbal communication sprinkled with the words "me" and "I love you" makes me laugh. My heart breaks with joy as three-year-old Jake calls me on the phone to tell me he misses me. I am lucky that they only live five minutes away and I can get an "Aunt Debbie fix" often. The older two - Benjamin and Samantha - are growing up so fast; he is now a teenager, she close behind. Benjamin calls me "cool Aunt Debbie": a name I wear proudly. I salute my siblings and all parents in fact. I understand how much work parenting truly is. The time I spend with the kids fulfills me and nurtures them, too. I also hope that the time off from parenting has helped create some added balance for my brother, sister, and their spouses.

I do a lot to create personal balance. I like spending time alone and make sure that I find time for rest and relaxation. I work out regularly, schedule bi-weekly manicures, a monthly pedicure, and a massage every few weeks. I also reward myself with spa days several times a year both at home and in faraway locales. I like to be pampered! Last year I put my physical endurance to the test by participating in the Avon 3 Day Breast Cancer walk with a dear friend who is a breast cancer survivor. We raised over $30,000 for breast cancer research and trained for months for a 60-mile walk. It was a rewarding experience that I will never forget.

I have also learned to walk away from the office to travel. Having never been to Europe, my 40th birthday present was a two-week trip to France. In the years that followed, I ventured twice to Italy and to Israel and Turkey with my parents (our first ever vacation together!). In recent years, I have chosen to stay closer to home, often scheduling long getaway weekends instead of weeklong trips. I even tested my cowgirl skills at a dude ranch in Colorado on a family vacation! Most importantly, when I do travel, I do not call into the office. I know when I can leave and schedule my time off accordingly. I am proud to say that I have learned how to leave work at work.

One thing that I know to be important is how to say no with confidence as well as how to say yes to myself! I have come to believe that none of us can do it all, at least not all at the same time. Learning to say no is key to living a balanced life. I have also come to accept that there is no such thing as perfect balance. Sometimes it is one step forward and two steps back. And I revel in the joy that that one step forward brings.

Writing this book has been in celebration of living a balanced life. It gives me great joy to share what I have learned. I know my balance in life will continue to change over time as my life changes. That is part of the mystery and magic that life has to offer. It is in adjusting to these changes that the celebration of life continues!

This book is intended to be a whimsical look at ideas that might help you in adding some balance to your life. As you read it, give yourself credit for everything that you already do. Make a wish list for future exploration. Some of the ideas will inspire you emotionally. Others might tug on your purse strings instead of your heartstrings. Some items will make you laugh. There is something to which everyone can and will relate.

Read the book from cover to cover or read it one page at a time, flipping to a page at random just for fun. Keep it next to your bed. Pack it in your suitcase when you travel. Share it with your girlfriends who are sure to relate to many of the concepts and suggestions found between the covers. Give this book as a gift. You can be sure it will be appreciated.

However you use it, just remember to allow balance to become a regular part of your existence. Your life balance will be whatever you allow it to be: whatever you choose to do or give to yourself. Balance is that which gives you peace of mind, calmness and serenity, a centered feeling of inner contentment. Balance is different for each and every one of us. What works for me will probably not be what works for you. Visualize what balance means to your life. And then take it one step at a time. Traveling the road to balance means learning to say yes to you.

You work hard and deserve the very best your life has to offer! Try not to forget that!

Balancing Notes

Work and Play

Learn to Delegate

- Assume personal responsibility with pride and ownership.

- Do not allow yourself to become entangled in a web of your own weaving.

- Let team members complement your skills.

- Organize and prioritize; everything will eventually get done!

It is not necessary to do it all, but
do well what you can!

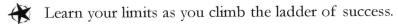

Establish Boundaries

✦ Learn your limits as you climb the ladder of success.

✦ Ask to what extent you are willing to sacrifice your personal life in order to achieve your professional goals.

✦ Realize - especially when you feel 'up against the wall' - that you have the power to enact change and set realistic boundaries.

✦ Locate the courage and confidence within to use your personal power to make necessary changes.

✦ Leave work at work!

Drive the scenic road to balance and live your life!

Save Money

★ Money can be fun to spend. It is more important to learn to live within your means.

★ Keep credit card debt to within reason.

★ List the many reasons you have to save... a special vacation, a new home, a car you've dreamed of driving, your child's education, your inevitable retirement, maybe just for a rainy day!

★ Learn your risk/reward comfort level when investing.

★ Budget savings into your financial plan even if it is only a few dollars a week.

Save for the future!

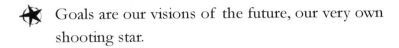

Have Goals

★ Goals are our visions of the future, our very own shooting star.

★ Goals provide a roadmap of your own making; a reason for being whether they are personal, professional, or financial, short-term or long-term, realistic or otherwise.

★ Goals change over time as you change.

★ Goals are the mirror reflection of who you are or who you want to be. Listen to your spirit as it speaks to you.

Look forward to the challenges that lie ahead!

Expand Your Horizons

★ Take a class and learn new things.

★ Stimulate your mind.

★ Cultivate a hobby: knit, sew, refinish furniture,
make handmade paper, sculpt ceramics, blow glass, or paint.

★ Ride a motorcycle, train for a marathon, cycle the trail.

★ Express your creative essence beyond the limits
of imagination.

★ Test your physical being.

★ Try new experiences. Focus on the enjoyment of doing.

If your hobby ever starts to feel like too
much of a chore, find a new hobby!

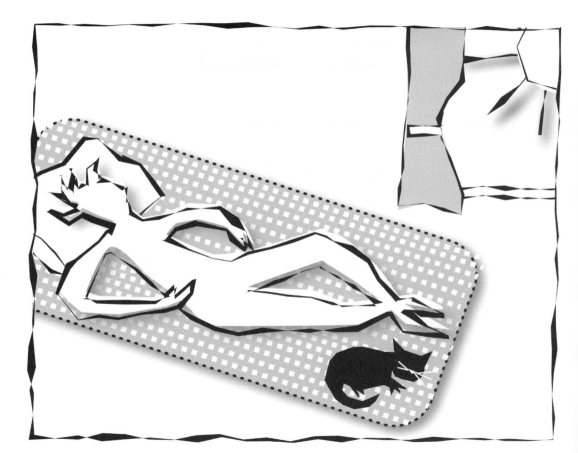

Indulge in a Nap

★ Stolen moments in the middle of the day.

★ Rest and respite in quiet solitude.

★ Energy replenished.

★ You are ready to tackle whatever the rest of your day might bring.

★ Anticipate being bright eyed and bushy tailed.

Now – go play well into the night!

Read a Good Book

★ Escape into the world of mystery, suspense, romance, adventure, and real life.

★ Curling up with a good book is therapy for the brain.

★ Learn about others and learn to help yourself.

★ Simply escape into fictional plots and characters created to entertain or perhaps even inspire.

★ Join a book club and share your thoughts and reactions.

★ Share books you enjoy with your friends.

Make time to read!

Enjoy a Lazy Day

⭐ Time to do what you want to do: nothing at all or everything at once.

⭐ A day to touch base at home, laze on the couch, read the newspaper, or tear through a novel.

⭐ A day to talk on the phone or pray it never rings.

⭐ A day to do laundry or catch up on bills.

⭐ A day to write a letter or surf the Net.

⭐ A day to rent videos, organize a photo album, sew on buttons, or watch sports on television for hours.

⭐ A day of your making, be it your "to do" list or simply a come-what-may day.

A day just for you!

Plan a Day at the Beach

★ Flirt with the tide as it ebbs and flows with the water rushing through the sand and seeping slowly through your toes. The breeze subdues the heat as the clouds masquerade the intensity of the sun's rays.

★ On a clear day, gaze into the seemingly endless horizon with wonder as the shimmering sun reflects brightly off the white sand.

★ Gather shells, make a sand castle, play in the water.

Remember to wear sunscreen!

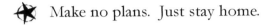

★ Make no plans. Just stay home.

★ Remind yourself that you even know how to cook!

★ Indulge yourself and order take-out or delivery.

★ Read a book, watch a video, cuddle with your honey, and forget your to-do list.

If your schedule seems to be "go-go-go", just kick back and stay at home!

Escape to a Hotel

★ Checkout the weekend specials. Run away from home for a night or two and check into a hotel.

★ Get on a plane or drive to the big city.

★ Fluff the pillows and take a nap.

★ Order room service and watch a movie.

★ Wrap the plush robe around you if one is among the amenities provided.

★ Take a long, luxurious bath.

★ Pack the little toiletries in your suitcase and take them home.

★ Sleep late and rest.

It's a mini-vacation!

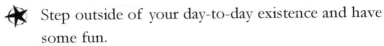

Permit Yourself a Long Weekend

✴ Step outside of your day-to-day existence and have some fun.

✴ Whether you are on the go or going nowhere, step back and let the days pass without a cell phone, beeper, or the woes that will still be there upon your return.

✴ Taking a few days for yourself sometimes feels like a week, energizing you to face whatever is on your agenda.

✴ A long weekend can also be a wake-up call for a real vacation.

Heed the call!

Take a Vacation

✸ Start off with a day, graduate to a long weekend, and soon you will thirst for the real thing: a week or perhaps even two weeks off.

✸ Whether you laze on a beach, trek through the country, ski the mountain, see the world, or simply play where you live, remember to take time to relax.

✸ Try to leave work at work in both spirit and deed.

✸ You will survive better if you can walk away and take some time for yourself.

Work will survive without you if you let it!

Savor a Glass of Wine

✸ Inhale the aroma.

✸ Taste the flavor of oak.

✸ Enjoy the sparkle of champagne and savor the fruit of the vine.

✸ Red or white; sweet or dry; a complement to your meal or a liquid treasure unto itself.

✸ Experiment with regional varieties.

✸ Become a connoisseur.

✸ Drink in moderation.

Share your discoveries with friends!

Drink Coffee, Tea, or ?

★ Wrap your hands around the warmth of the mug and watch the steam escape.

★ Drink your tea or coffee chilled, touching the glass to your forehead; allowing the water beads to drip against your skin.

★ Smell the beans; inhale the aroma.

★ Enjoy your liquid refreshment as day ends and becomes the edge of night.

★ Say no to nighttime caffeine and let sweet dreams find you as you nod off to sleep.

Savor the variety of flavors and relish the pureness of the blend!

Let the Music Move You

★ Jazz, classical, new age, blues, country, or good old rock 'n roll... whether vocal or instrumental, the tones and rhythms soothe the soul and feed your spirit.

★ Get your feet a-tappin' and let your body start to sway as the beat weaves its path to your inner ear and manifests itself physically.

★ Let your mind drift and just move to the music of the day or night.

Music adds variety and a spice to life!

Do a Dance

★ Clap your hands and tap your feet.

★ Hear the music, feel the beat.

★ Shake your booty, don't be shy.

★ Put on your dancing shoes; let your body fly.

★ Dance fast or dance slow.

★ Move with the pulse as the music flows.

You've got the rhythm. Let it show!

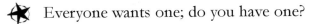

**Let Someone Else
Clean Your House**

- Everyone wants one; do you have one?
- Time is money and money well spent might include hiring a cleaning service.
- You will always need to straighten up before they come but, weekly, bi-weekly, or even monthly, the luxury of a cleaning pro doing this necessary but dreaded chore is well worth it.
- However you spend those "extra" hours not cleaning, don't forget to smile when you walk into your house and inhale the lingering fresh clean scent.

You work hard! You deserve to come home
to a clean house now and then!

Balancing Notes

Friends and Family

Share a Hug

◈ A greeting with affection.

◈ Arms lightly wrapped around you: a caring touch of love and support.

◈ A big bearhold that ensnares you, lifting you up physically as well as emotionally.

◈ A simple pleasure that inspires feelings of warmth and goodwill.

Share them freely!

Phone a Friend

◆ You may not win a million dollars, but you will feel like a million bucks!

◆ Who but a good friend knows just how to make you laugh or lets you bare all without judging you?

◆ Sometimes, simply hearing their voice is just what the doctor ordered.

Phone a friend and you will
be pleased when they phone, too!

Cherish Friends

◈ Friends are the people we choose to love: a person to talk to or someone to play with.

◈ Friends laugh with you and even sometimes at you in that true friend spirit.

◈ They are always there to provide a shoulder to cry on or offer needed words of encouragement at just the right moment.

◈ Open yourself up to all the joy and warmth that good friends bring to your life!

You will not regret it!

Reconnect with an Old Friend

◈ Years pass and friendships fade, the reasons no longer clear in your mind or even important.

◈ A childhood friend, a college roommate, a coffee klatch compatriot from a former job or a neighbor long since moved away.

◈ Make the first effort to reconnect. Pick up the phone, write a note, or use a modem to find them online.

◈ Catch up as if it was yesterday.

◈ Smile when you remember just why you were friends.

◈ Promise each other not to lose touch for so long again.

Work to keep that promise!

Give and Receive Love

◈ Open your heart and let love into your life.

◈ Love yourself first without becoming selfish and self-centered.

◈ Love your neighbors as well as your friends.

◈ Seek out and enjoy an emotionally healthy relationship with a partner who is responsive to your needs and with whom you can reciprocate accordingly.

◈ Don't confuse love and sex.

Rejoice when the loving is lovely!

Coordinate Family Time

- ◈ Sunday dinner, family meetings, quality time as a cohesive family unit.
- ◈ Communicate yet try not to argue.
- ◈ Learn to respect one another's opinions.
- ◈ Acknowledge each other's strengths and weaknesses.
- ◈ Remember that you were a child before you became a parent.
- ◈ Look at life through the eyes of a child.
- ◈ Empathize with the growing pains of adolescence and celebrate the adventures of becoming an adult.
- ◈ Glow when given the gift of grandchildren!

Relish the simple joys of day-to-day family existence!

◆ Time passes and patterns emerge in relationships. Schedule a date and take the time to play together.

◆ Reminisce about times before there were kids or the stresses of a busy life.

◆ Keep the doors open and communicate.

◆ Remember that "for better or worse" doesn't always have to mean better. Celebrate life when it does!

Plan time together so that you will stay together!

Arrange a Girl's Night Out

◈ An evening just for the girls; often revolving around some kind of meal or in celebration of a special occasion.

◈ A night on the town or in the comfort of someone's home.

◈ Laughing, sharing and telling the stories of sisterhood make you plan the next get-together before evening's end.

The opportunity to spend quality time with your girlfriends is a special event itself!

Cook a Meal

◈ Explore a cookbook or cooking magazine.

◈ Select a new recipe to try.

◈ Experiment on yourself or invite friends.

◈ Be realistic about the time and effort you really want to put into the meal.

◈ Buy ingredients you have never used before.

◈ Read the instructions with consideration and care.

Eat slowly and savor the fruits of your labor!

Delight in Fun Dining

- ◈ Try a trendy new restaurant or return to an old family favorite. Fancy, funky, or blue jean casual does not matter.

- ◈ Clear your palette and prepare yourself for a culinary experience.

- ◈ Savor the tastes.

- ◈ Admire the presentation, the colors in compliment of food and courses.

- ◈ Be adventurous and order something unique. Or go with your tried-and-true favorite that is always sure to please.

- ◈ Call for reservations.

- ◈ Open your wallet for that special occasion.

Dine in style!

Honor Your Parents

- You are the fruit of their lives and have been the apple of their eye from the day of your birth.
- As you age, don't let your independence interfere with establishing an adult relationship with your parents.
- Forgive them for their shortcomings for they too, are human.
- Acknowledge their sacrifices when bringing you up.
- Don't wait for health issues to rob them of the quality of life or threaten their mortality.

Treat your parents with the respect
and love they deserve!

Reach Out to a Child

◆ All children are our future.

◆ Love your offspring unconditionally.

◆ Let your spiritual foundation and emotional guidance build confidence and teach right from wrong.

◆ Influence the life of a child just by being a family friend, a loving aunt, or a volunteer big sister.

◆ Read to a toddler or take a friend's child to see the newest animated movie.

◆ Let a teenager know you are there for them in times of trouble; just a phone call away.

The rewards are reflected in their knowing
smiles and your caring heart!

Snap a Picture

◈ They always abound, although we seem to remember them most often on special occasions and vacations.

◈ Capture the moment: snap it, frame it, and share the results with family and friends.

◈ Create keepsake albums.

◈ Remember to look back at your pictures to recall times gone by, happy doings, good friends, and the everyday special moments of life!

A picture really is worth a thousand words!

Write a Letter

◈ In our always evolving, fast-paced age of electronic media and communication, the art of letter writing seems long forgotten.

◈ "Snail mail" brings great joy to the recipient who can't help but smile in pleasant surprise.

◈ Take the time to send out a card or a letter.

◈ Enclose a picture.

◈ Acknowledge an occasion.

◈ Say thank-you.

Remind someone that you care!

Throw a Party

◈ Always the guest and never the hostess? Find an occasion or create one.

◈ Design a theme party.

◈ Have it at home or rent out a special space.

◈ Send out formal invitations or simply pick up the phone.

◈ Have it catered or show off your culinary skills.

Formal or casual, night or day,
celebrate just your way!

Balancing Notes

Heart & Soul

Just Say No!

♥ A little two-letter word that is easy to say to your kids, yet difficult to say to anyone else.

♥ Remind yourself often that you don't have to be super-woman or super-mom.

♥ Remember that "no" is "on" spelled backwards. You don't always have to be "on"!

♥ Trust your intuition and say "no" when "yes" stems from an innate sense of guilt or obligation.

♥ The freedom and courage to say "no" will give you the strength and renewed energy to feel "on" when you need it most.

When you learn to say "no", you will then be able to say "yes" with pleasure when "yes" is your heart's desire!

Cultivate a Positive Attitude

♥ See the glass as half full and not half empty.

♥ Keep your chin up and go with the flow.

♥ Live with PMA instead of PMS.

♥ A positive mental attitude helps even the keel and keeps you going and growing stronger for the long haul which is life.

There is nothing to be gained in being negative, so simply try to be positive!

Laugh a Lot

♥ Laugh at a joke, an amusing anecdote, and sometimes even at yourself.

♥ Laugh out loud.

♥ Laugh yourself silly.

♥ Share the mood and enjoy the moment for everything it is... and isn't.

Whether a deep belly roar, an infectious giggle, or a cheery chuckle, laughing is good for the soul!

Know How to Listen

♥ Good communication requires not just talking but listening, too.

♥ Hear what someone really has to say and is truly asking for.

♥ Wait before responding even though the natural temptation is to reply in turn, often interrupting before the thought is even complete.

♥ What you give in life, you get back.

Learn to listen and you, in turn, will be heard!

Clean Your Closets

- ❤ Sort out excess hangers from trips to the dry cleaner and unworn clothes accumulating in an unorganized fashion.

- ❤ Tag gifts for the giving and boxes and papers for wrapping, which are often scattered on shelves in a haphazard mess.

- ❤ Unclutter your life and periodically clean out your closets.

- ❤ If you haven't worn it in three years, take a deep breath and purge it.

- ❤ Donate the goodies and be charitable in your endeavor.

- ❤ Make it a seasonal task.

Find amazing new space and long lost treasures!

Shop 'Til You Drop

- ♥ Browse through the stores perusing the newest fashions.

- ♥ Be brave! Try on something you'd never dare to wear.

- ♥ Check out the sale rack and take pride in your bargains.

- ♥ If a gift calls out to you, purchase it and start a gift shelf.

- ♥ Head to the mall or an urban street full of fun boutiques.

- ♥ Never abuse your credit cards to indulge a whim.

- ♥ Make a day of it or satisfy yourself in just an hour.

Unpack your treasures with glee!

Grow a Garden

- ♥ Buds emerge from deep beneath the earth's surface. The plants bloom in turn; a well-timed orchestra of birth and renewal in vivid color.

- ♥ Grow vegetables and lovingly harvest the fruits of your labor.

- ♥ Weed with tender loving care.

- ♥ Contemplate, meditate, and communicate with your environment.

- ♥ Nurture nature.

- ♥ Turn your green space into a tranquil oasis.

Enjoy the splendorous results!

Celebrate Your Birthday

❤ If you don't celebrate the day you were born, who should?

❤ Celebrate another year of life.

❤ Accept that you are getting older.

❤ Acknowledge that with age has come wisdom.

❤ Have fun.

❤ Eat cake.

❤ Buy yourself a present.

Take special care to make it a special day!

Appreciate the Beauty of Flowers

❤ Appreciate the exotic beauty, the colorful display, and aromatic fragrances that escape from the blooms.

❤ Watch each day as buds blossom and grow.

❤ Give them as a gift to yourself to merely celebrate the day: no special occasion required.

❤ Press the best petals between the pages of your favorite book and enjoy the memories when you reread that favorite passage.

Let flowers surround you with grace and beauty!

Calm Yourself with Candles

♥ The flickering flames, the scent of essential oils, the asymmetric patterns of the burning wax. Lighting candles has always been a ritual reserved for celebrating holidays.

♥ Now a custom of relaxation: several burning at once, a room lit merely by the presence of the glowing wicks and patterns of light dancing in the darkness.

♥ As the candles glow, let your imagination wish at will.

Let candles set the mood as you relax and reflect!

Light a Fire

❤ Logs crackle as their flames dance before your eyes.

❤ Gather in the warmth.

❤ Let the illumination envelop you on a cold or damp day,
as day turns to dusk and dusk becomes darkness.

Light a fire and let the spirit within you

leap with the flames!

Play it by Ear

♥ Not everything is meant to be planned.

♥ Sometimes, you have to be spontaneous and do something whimsical - something last minute that you may not have even thought of until that very moment.

♥ Sometimes, it means "wait and see", giving yourself a chance to see how the day goes without a commitment to the clock or a preordained schedule.

♥ Make decisions as the day unfolds.

Put aside your schedule for the day and see what happens!

Be Charitable

♥ Give of your time or open your checkbook.

♥ The amount of your gift is not important.

♥ Small acts of kindness stem from goodness.

♥ Support a cause that touches your heart.

♥ Charitable giving is the stepping-stone for research and results.

♥ Acknowledge that those less fortunate need your help.

Know that your reward is in the giving!

Volunteer Your Time

♥ Give of yourself to those in need.

♥ Believe in a cause and champion it into result-oriented action.

♥ Serve on a board and strut your stuff.

♥ Use your skills and talents to benefit an organization's fulfillment and purpose.

♥ Do merely because doing gives you a gratified sense of fulfillment and purpose.

♥ Expect nothing in return.

Your rewards will be great!

Schedule a Day of Rest

♥ Choose your day to rest, reflect, and relax!

♥ A real day of rest recharges your batteries and renews you for whatever lies ahead.

♥ If you must work or do chores, try not to rush.

♥ This special day each week shouldn't be about rushing. Doing, perhaps. Rushing, no.

Choose to spend your day your way!

Have Faith

- ❤ Believe in a higher being.

- ❤ Let your sense of faith guide you and enlighten you in your quest for meaning and purpose.

- ❤ Don't judge others if their beliefs differ from yours.

- ❤ Treat others as you want to be treated.

- ❤ Learn the difference between right and wrong and then absorb the meanings.

- ❤ Allow hope to enter boldly into your heart.

- ❤ Choose to be a good person.

Live what you learn about yourself and others!

Keep a Journal

♥ Record your innermost thoughts, goals, and feelings in a notebook created and saved just for you.

♥ Draw, create, doodle, dream, and map your plans in your journal's safe pages.

♥ Keep it next to your bed or hidden in a secret drawer.

♥ Pack it in your suitcase when you travel.

♥ Whether you make daily entries or write on a whim, keeping a journal gives credence to your feelings as they come to the forefront of your mind.

♥ Periodically reread what you wrote.

Allow your journal to help you learn about yourself and grow!

Be Alone

- Step back and just be alone with yourself, alone with your thoughts.

- Give your partner space to enable them to experience similar solitude.

- Do you truly like the company you keep in those empty moments?

- Explore who you are and do not fear the answers.

- Moments of peace and quiet are pearls in your own treasure chest of gems: self-discovery, self confidence, and self-renewal.

Take the necessary time to simply be you!

Balancing Notes

Mind & Body

Listen to Your Body

- We age and our bodies start to betray us: aches and pains we never noticed, lumps that shouldn't be there.

- Heed the call when your body *does* ask for help and seek medical advice and attention.

- Get annual check-ups and timely mammograms.

- Go to the dentist.

- Make an appointment for an eye exam.

- Do not take good health for granted.

Honor your body!

Eat Healthy

- If you are what you eat, then eating healthy may just keep you living the good life longer.

- Eat fruits and vegetables regularly.

- Watch your caloric and fat intake.

- Eat a balanced diet and don't intentionally skip meals.

- Try to stay away from junk food.

- Know how your body reacts to carbohydrates and protein. Adjust your diet accordingly.

- Eat more chicken and fish instead of red meat. Indulge your sweet tooth in moderation.

- Eat to sustain yourself.

Enjoy what you eat!

Dress Up

- Forget your blue jeans, spandex leggings, or day-to-day business attire.

- Take out your party dress or dressy outfit and dress to the nines.

- Whether for a wedding or just for kicks, accessorize with that funky jewelry, glittery eye shadow, new shade of lipstick, and dab of perfume.

- Look in the mirror and smile at your pretty self.

Now go out and have a good time!

Breathe Deeply

- Close your eyes and take a deep, bottom-of-the-lung breath.

- Inhale. Exhale. Now do it again.

- You are always in motion, unaware of your racing heart.

- Make an effort to calm the stress by taking a deep, deep breath.

- Let the conscious process relax you.

Stop and savor the moment!

Value Daily Rituals

◎ Indulge in the splendor of a daily ritual that makes *you* feel good about *you.*

◎ Step out of a hot shower and apply lotion all over your body. Let your body lovingly absorb the splendid ingredients and your delicate touch!

◎ Place a dab of perfume in your secret place to release just a hint of a smile.

◎ Don coordinating jewelry to match your mood, not just your outfit.

Relish the joy that these simple pleasures invoke!

Bathe Luxuriously

◉ Listen as warm water flows from the spigot while bubbles cascade around you.

◉ Permit the stress to release from your body as you let yourself sink into the depth of the tub.

◉ During your luxurious float, indulge yourself with simple bath products that smell good and make you feel like the princess that you are allowing yourself to be.

Allow the embryonic rhythm of the water to transport you out to sea, miles away from your woes!

Treat Yourself to a Manicure

- Buff, file, soak, shape, paint.

- Short nails suddenly look longer, talons existing to highlight your unique personality.

- Reasonably priced so you can treat yourself weekly, bi-weekly, or even just for special occasions.

- Coordinate colors with your clothes or lips or maybe just your mood of the moment!

Give yourself this simple indulgence that makes your hands look and feel marvelous!

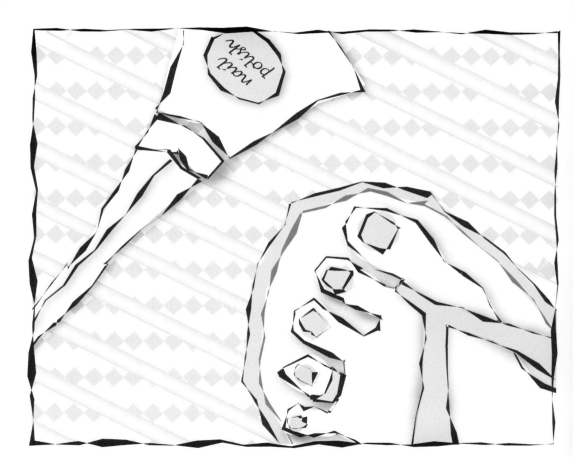

Step Out for a Pedicure

- Get to know the rich cousin to the manicure; think feet.

- An indulgence that makes toes stand out in your summer sandals, barefoot on the beach, or even cooped up inside winter soles.

- We abuse our feet. They sweat and get tired and dry. We often don't honor them until they scream for attention.

- A ritual that, if performed monthly, keeps your walking digits dreaming lazily of their next soapy vibrating journey to the footbath.

Pamper with a pedicure -
Your feet will thank you!

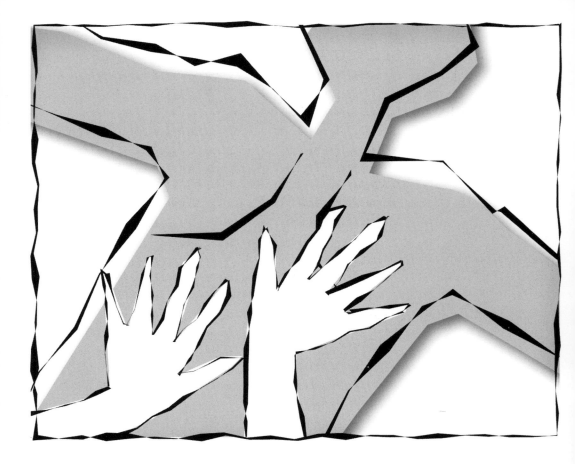

Relax with a Massage

- Touching hands, healing hands.

- The art of stretching sore and tired muscles.

- The temporary release of accumulated stress.

- Learning to respond to your body's needs in a positive and healthy way.

- Trusting hands to help, not hurt, even though some times the pain is the best, most healing release.

Relax and indulge your body with a massage!

Submerge in a Spa Day

- ◎ Renewal, rejuvenation, relaxation.

- ◎ The earned rewards of a job well done or a present to yourself.

- ◎ Nurture your spirit, body, and soul.

- ◎ Pamper yourself.

- ◎ With this newfound energy, you will embrace a new day, a new horizon, awaiting the magic and mystery of what life will bring next.

Treat yourself! You deserve it!

Get a New 'Do'

- Cut your hair or let it grow long.

- Change the color or just add highlights.

- Make it curly or iron it straight.

- Check out the latest styles in a fashion magazine.

Take a beauty safari and smile back
at that new you in the mirror!

Be Sure to Exercise

- Let the endorphins settle in your brain and clear your consciousness while sweat drips from your pores.

- Walk, ride, run, swim, take an aerobics class, or lift weights.

- What you do for exercise does not matter. What does matter is that you exercise on a regular basis.

- Join a club or workout in the privacy of your home.

- Tone your body, strengthen your heart, live better and longer.

Exercise your body and the big surprise will be
renewed energy for all of your life's endeavors!

Participate in a Sport

- Get some exercise, chat with friends, and get your competitive juices going.

- Golf, tennis, volleyball, baseball, football, hockey, soccer, racquetball, squash, or even curling!

- Team against team, player against player.

- Learn to play together in sport and after-sport.

- Bask in the thrill of victory and be gracious in the agony of defeat.

- Cheer your team.

- Never boo your opponent.

Play a sport, be a sport!

Go For a Walk

- On the beach, in your neighborhood, scattering leaves in the woods, or in a light misting rain.

- Appreciate your surroundings on the balls of your feet instead of the seat of your pants.

- Be good to your feet and wear appropriate shoes.

- Be good to your heart and increase the pace.

- Push the stroller, walk the dog, think, or talk.

Alone or with company,
enjoy the view and have fun too!

Experience Nature

- Take a walk in the woods, tend to your garden, hike up a mountain, or sleep in a tent.

- Explore the wonder of the big outdoors.

- Relish the change of seasons... the buds on the trees and first flowers of spring, the flowing waters of summer, the colors of fall.

- A fresh layer of snow coating the grass, unspoiled by movement until daybreak.

Commune with nature and just be!

Balancing Notes

Epilogue – Your Balancing Activities

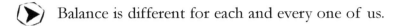

Things to Remember

▶ Balance is different for each and every one of us.

▶ Finding the road to balance will require continuous adjustment to constant change.

▶ Balance will not be achieved overnight.

▶ Integrate balancing activities into your life one step at a time.

▶ Balance may need to be scheduled into your life just like a business meeting!

▶ Strive for reasonable balance in the long run.

(There is no such thing as perfect balance!

Beat the Clock Activities

 Things You Can Do With an Hour or Two

indulge in a nap... read a good book... savor a glass of wine... drink coffee, tea, or ?... let the music move you... do a dance... share hugs... phone a friend... snap a photo... write a letter... laugh a lot... know how to listen... appreciate the beauty of flowers... calm yourself with candles... play it by ear... keep a journal... be alone... dress up... breathe deeply... value daily rituals... bathe luxuriously...treat yourself to a manicure... step out for a pedicure... relax with a massage... get a new 'do'... be sure to exercise... go for a walk... experience nature...

 Things To Do With an Afternoon, Evening, or Whole Day

enjoy a lazy day... plan a day at the beach... stay home on Saturday night... escape to a hotel... reconnect with an old friend... schedule family time... arrange a girls night out... cook a meal... delight in fine dining... throw a party... clean your closets... shop 'til you drop... light a fire... volunteer your time... submerge in a spa day... participate in a sport...

Take time for balance!

Free Balancing Activities... or Less Than $20

indulge in a nap... read a good book... enjoy a lazy day... plan a day at the beach... savor a glass of wine... drink coffee, tea, or ?... let the music move you... share hugs... phone a friend... honor your parents... reach out to a child... write a letter... just say no!... cultivate a positive attitude... laugh a lot... know how to listen... appreciate the beauty of flowers... calm yourself with candles... volunteer your time... schedule a day of rest... have faith... keep a journal... be alone... breathe deeply... value daily rituals... bathe luxuriously... treat yourself to a manicure... go for a walk...

Participate in balancing activities
that don't cost a lot of money!

Activities to Do Alone

 Just for You and Yourself

establish boundaries… save money… have goals… expand your horizons… indulge in a nap… read a good book… enjoy a lazy day… plan a day at the beach… stay home on Saturday night… escape to a hotel… permit yourself a long weekend… take a vacation… savor a glass of wine… drink coffee, tea, or ?… let the music move you… let someone else clean your house… cook a meal… write a letter… just say no!… cultivate a positive attitude… laugh a lot… clean your closets… shop 'til you drop… grow a garden… celebrate your birthday… appreciate the beauty of flowers… calm yourself with candles… light a fire… play it by ear… be charitable… volunteer your time… schedule a day of rest… have faith… keep a journal… be alone… listen to your body… eat healthy… dress up… breathe deeply… value daily rituals… bathe luxuriously… treat yourself to a manicure… step out for a pedicure… relax with a massage… submerge in a spa day… get a new 'do'… be sure to exercise… go for a walk… experience nature…

For Balance with Another

learn to delegate… do a dance… share hugs… phone a friend… cherish friends… reconnect with an old friend…give and receive love…plan a date with the love of your life…schedule a girls night out…delight in fun dining… honor your parents… reach out to a child… snap a photo… know how to listen… participate in a sport…

Remember, many of the things you can do
for and by yourself will be even more
fun to do with two!

List some of the balancing acts that you have already made a part
of your day-to day life.

1.
2.
3.
4.
5.
6.
7.
8.
9.

Now, give yourself a pat on the back and a round of applause
for all the things you already do so well!

Your Balance Wish List

 List some of the balancing acts that spoke to you, that called your name and begged to be tried. At this point don't worry if they are entirely realistic or whether you can afford them.

1.
2.
3.
4.
5.
6.
7.
8.
9.

Just dream! Wishes can come true!

Your Daily Balance Sheet

Sometimes you need to hold yourself accountable! This daily balance sheet is intended to help you organize your thoughts and actions. By just taking a few minutes each day, you will find yourself on the road to balance with less interference from the traffic of your day-to-day life!

1. Which balancing act do you plan to do today? Write it down here.

2. Is there a balancing act you want to do today? Make a commitment in writing.

3. What would you do for yourself today with an extra 15 minutes?

4. Is there a balancing act you need to schedule this week?
    For next week?   For next month?

5. Is there a friend you have been thinking about and have
    been meaning to call?

6. Do you have something fun to read?

7. What would you do as a treat for yourself if you had an
    extra $50?

By writing it down, you take a step beyond mere thought.
You make it real!

Your Strategic Balance Plan

▶ Pick five things from your Balance Wish List that you think you can (and will) integrate into your life.

▶ Assign target dates!

▶ Be realistic with yourself!

▶ Pick one thing to achieve in the next week and then one to achieve in the next month. Choose whatever is going to work for you and set some balance goals!

▶ Review your plan periodically. Update it for changes you have already made and new changes you wish to implement!

Most importantly, have fun!
Enjoy all that your life has to offer!

Your Strategic Balance Plan Target Chart

1.
Target Date

2.
Target Date

3.
Target Date

4.
Target Date

5.
Target Date

Cleaning Service

Name
Phone

Favorite Fancy Restaurant

Name
Phone

Favorite Family Restaurant

Name
Phone

Favorite Delivery Restaurant

Name
Phone

Babysitter

Name
Phone

Your Balance Directory

Florist

Name

Phone

Hairdresser

Name

Phone

Manicurist

Name

Phone

Health Club

Name

Phone

Doctor

Name

Phone

Balancing Notes

Life is a Balancing Act... a fun book is Debbie Lessin's first book. She lives her balanced life in Chicago, Illinois. You can write to Debbie through her website – www.lifeisabalancingact.com.